J
Biography Lawson, Don.
Reagan   The picture life of Ronald Reagan /
            by Don Lawson. -- New York : F. Watts,
            1981.
                48 p. : ill.   bfc 3-5

                SUMMARY: Highlights the life of the
            40th President from his childhood
            through his years as a movie actor to
            the White House.
                ISBN 0-531-04286-3 : 6.90

            1.Reagan, Ronald. 2.Presidents.

60592

80-29085 N81
          MARC AC

The Picture Life of
RONALD REAGAN

THE PICTURE LIFE OF
Ronald Reagan

BY DON LAWSON

FRANKLIN WATTS

New York/London/Toronto/Sydney

1981

**Frontispiece: the president
gets a victory kiss
from daughter Maureen.
He has just learned
that he won the election.**

Library of Congress Cataloging in Publication Data

Lawson, Don.
The picture life of Ronald Reagan

Includes index.
SUMMARY: Highlights the life of the
40th President from his childhood through his
years as a movie actor to the White House.
1. Reagan, Ronald — Juvenile literature.
2. Presidents — United States —
Biography — Juvenile literature.
[1. Reagan, Ronald. 2. Presidents]   I. Title.
E877.L38   973.927′092′4 [B] [92]   80-29085
ISBN 0-531-04286-3

JAN   4 1982

R. L. 2.8 Spache Revised Formula   C.98

Photographs courtesy of
United Press International: frontis, pp. 6 (bottom),
9, 23, 24, 27, 46 (far left);
Wide World Photos: pp. 6 (top), 11,
12, 16 (left), 19, 20, 28, 33, 34,
37, 38, 40 (both), 41, 43, 46 (right), and 47;
The Reagan Campaign '80: pp. 8, 15,
16 (right), 31, and 44 (Roger Sandler).

The Picture Life of
RONALD REAGAN

Ronald Reagan is the fortieth president of the United States. He is the first movie and TV star to become president.

Most presidents have been lawyers. Some have been soldiers. Others have been teachers, engineers, or businessmen. One was even a tailor. Jimmy Carter was the president before Reagan. He was a peanut farmer.

Top: his family watches on TV as Reagan becomes a candidate for president. Below: the president-elect and his wife wave to the crowd. It is Reagan's first appearance after the election.

But no other president has been an actor.

Ronald Reagan had other jobs, too, before becoming president. He was the governor of California. He was also the president of the Screen Actors Guild. This is a large union most movie actors belong to. Another job Ronald Reagan had was working for the General Electric Company.

Ronald Reagan, movie star. The photograph at right is from the film *Juke Girl*. The one on the left is from *The Knute Rockne Story*.

Ronald Reagan is the oldest man ever to become president of the United States. He was sixty-nine when he was elected. He turned seventy only a few weeks after he took office.

But President Reagan looks like a much younger man. He has dark brown hair. Some people say he dyes his hair to keep it from going gray. But Reagan says this isn't true. He says his hair has stayed brown in spite of his age.

President Reagan likes to exercise. One way he exercises is by riding horses. He once said, "There is nothing so good for the inside of a man as the outside of a horse."

President Reagan and his wife, Nancy, own a 688-acre ranch near Santa Barbara, California. When he is at the ranch, Reagan keeps in shape by cutting firewood and building fences.

Reagan relaxing and getting some exercise at his ranch.

Ronald Wilson Reagan was born on February 6, 1911, in the small town of Tampico, Illinois. His parents were John and Nellie (Wilson) Reagan. There was one other child in the family. This was Neil. Neil is two years older than Ronald.

The Reagan family was poor. John, the father, was a shoe salesman. He did not make much money. Because of this the family moved around a lot. They lived in several different small Illinois towns. For a short time they also lived in Chicago. But they stayed poor.

Ronald Reagan later said, "Sometimes we got by for a week on a ten-cent soup bone and some liver that my mother begged from the butcher. She told the butcher it was for our cat."

The John Reagan family.
Ronald is the shorter of
the two boys.

It was Nellie Reagan who kept the family together. She once worked in a dress shop to help support the family. Her pay was $14 a week. She fought hard to keep the children from feeling poor. Somehow she succeeded.

"I guess we were poor, all right," Ronald Reagan said. "But because of my mother we never knew it."

Ronald's older brother Neil was called "Moon." When Ronald started grade school in Monmouth, Illinois, he also had a nickname. It was "Dutch." Moon called his brother Dutch, he said, because Ronald was a "sissy" name. It was his father, though, who first gave Ronald the nickname.

Ronald when he was approximately twelve years old.

Donald Reagan
"Dutch"

"Life is just one grand sweet song, so start the music."

Pres. N. S. Student Body 4; Pres. 2; Play 3, 4; Dram. Club 3, 4, Pres. 4; Fresh.-Soph. Drama Club 1, 2, Pres. 2; Football 3, 4; Annual Staff; Hi-Y 3, 4, Vice-Pres. 4; Art. 1, 2; Lit. Contest 2; Track 2, 3.

Dutch Reagan was a small boy. When he was in high school in Dixon he was only 5 feet 3 inches (1.58 m) tall. He weighed only 108 pounds (49 kg). He also wore big glasses with heavy rims. He hated them. Today, President Reagan stands just over 6 feet (1.8 m) tall and weighs about 185 pounds (84 kg). He wears contact lenses instead of glasses.

Even though he was small, Dutch Reagan went out for football in both high school and college. "He was no star," Reagan's football coach said. "But he made up in fight what he lacked in size."

Opposite, top: the Dixon, Illinois, High School yearbook. Here Ronald is a senior. The name Donald is a mistake.
Opposite, bottom: Dutch Reagan during college football practice.

Reagan graduated from Dixon High School in 1928. He went to Eureka College in Eureka, Illinois. He earned some of the money for school by washing dishes at a fraternity house. During summer vacations he earned $18 a week as a lifeguard. He also had a scholarship.

Besides athletics Ronald was also interested in politics and acting. He was president of his class. He belonged to the college drama club and acted in several plays. When he graduated from Eureka in 1932, he decided to try and find a job as a radio actor.

But the only radio job he could get was as a sports announcer. His first radio job was in Davenport, Iowa. Davenport is just across the Mississippi River from Dixon, Illinois. His pay was $10 a game. Reagan was popular in Davenport. Soon the radio station WHO in Des Moines, Iowa, hired him for $75 a week.

Ronald Reagan working as a sportscaster for WHO radio.

Dutch Reagan became the most popular sports announcer WHO ever had. But he still wanted to act. In the spring of 1937 he was in California. He was with the Chicago Cubs baseball team. The Cubs were on a spring training trip to the West Coast. Between radio broadcasts back to Iowa, Reagan took a screen test at one of the Hollywood movie studios. As soon as he saw the test, Jack Warner of Warner Brothers Studio signed Reagan to an acting contract. He was to be paid $200 a week. The small-town boy from Illinois was on his way.

When Reagan signed his contract with Warner Brothers, this photograph was released. It shows him working as a lifeguard during college.

Over the next twenty years Ronald Reagan acted in more than fifty movies. He also married a Hollywood actress named Jane Wyman. They had met in the studio cafeteria. They were married in 1940. Jane and Ronald had two children. One was a daughter, Maureen, born in 1941. The other was a son, Michael, whom they adopted in 1945.

Most of the early movies Ronald Reagan acted in were not very good. They were called "B" movies. But he was popular with movie audiences. Soon he got a chance to act in better films. One top-rated film he was in was called *King's Row* (1941). It was about life in a small town.

Jane and Ronald
with their two children.

But just around that time the United States got into World War II. Reagan joined the Army Air Corps in April 1942. He did not become a flyer though. His eyesight was too poor. Instead, he made movies that were used to teach other men how to fly planes. These were called "training films." He became a captain in the Air Corps. When the war ended in 1945, he went back to acting.

"Captain" Ronald Reagan with his wife, Jane, at a movie opening.

From 1947 to 1952, and again in 1959 and early 1960, Reagan was president of the Screen Actors Guild. He led the union in its efforts to help actors who were too old or too sick to work. He got medical insurance and pensions for some union members who had none. He also got better benefits for those who were already covered.

In the late 1940s, Reagan's life and career took a bad turn. He couldn't get any good parts to play in the movies. And in 1948, Jane Wyman divorced him.

Reagan during his days as president of the Screen Actors Guild. He is seen here speaking before Congress.

But soon things began to look brighter. Television became popular in the 1950s. Reagan got acting roles in TV plays. He also became the host of two TV series. These were "Death Valley Days" and the "General Electric Theater."

Here Reagan is shown acting in a 1961 episode of "The General Electric Theater."

In 1952, Reagan married another actress, Nancy Davis. Nancy and Ronald had two children. A daughter, Patricia Ann, was born in 1953. A son, Ronald Prescott, was born in 1958.

About this time Reagan took a job that started him on his road to the presidency. He was hired by the General Electric Company (GE) to talk to workers in GE offices and factories. He was supposed to improve relations between the workers and management. He gave the workers "pep talks." He told them, "Progress is our most important product." This was a famous slogan of GE's. Reagan believed strongly in progress. He felt that progress in industry was the key to America's future. The workers also enjoyed hearing Reagan tell stories about Hollywood.

**Ronald Reagan marries
Nancy Davis.**

Soon Reagan began to add politics to his talks. He was against "big government," he said. He wanted the government to stop spending so much money. He said the government interfered too much with the movie industry, for example. Before long, he said, the government would be trying to run GE.

The people at GE liked Reagan's political talks. They told him he ought to run for public office. Then he could put his political ideas to work.

In the 1960s, Reagan became active in the California Republican party. In 1964, he made a speech in favor of Arizona Senator Barry Goldwater. Goldwater was the Republican candidate for president of the United States. Reagan's speech was on TV. Once again he spoke out against big government trying to run everything. People should be free to run their lives and businesses the way they wanted to,

Reagan said. Republicans across the country agreed. Goldwater lost the election, but everybody remembered Reagan's speech.

In 1966, Reagan ran for governor of California. He was supported by several wealthy California businessmen. Reagan won the election by almost a million votes. One of his millionaire backers said Reagan would be the next president of the United States. The new governor just laughed at this.

The new governor of California is sworn in.

Many people in California thought Reagan did a good job during his two terms in office. He did not cut government spending as much as he said he would. But he cut it some. And almost everybody agreed that Reagan was an honest governor. He was well-liked also, as he had been when he was a movie star. When he left office in 1974, a California newspaper said, "Reagan left the state in much better shape than he found it."

Ronald Reagan signs his first bill as governor of California.

In 1976, former Governor Reagan decided to run for the presidency. But he lost the Republican party's nomination to Gerald R. Ford. Ford was already president. He was running for reelection. The Democratic party's nominee was Jimmy Carter. Carter defeated Ford and became the nation's thirty-ninth president in January 1977.

Ronald Reagan talking to former President Gerald R. Ford.

Most people thought that Reagan had lost his chance to become president. He would be too old to run in 1980, they said. But Reagan fooled them. One of his friends said, "He never stopped running." In November 1979, Reagan announced he would run again in 1980.

On the campaign trail. **Reagan talks to construction workers, farmers (over left), and many others about his ideas on how to run the government. Over right: candidate Reagan enjoys an evening out with one of his supporters, singer Frank Sinatra.**

Six other Republicans also tried to get the nomination for president. But Reagan defeated them all. The man who gave Reagan the toughest fight was George Bush. After Reagan was nominated in Detroit in July 1980, he chose Bush to run with him as his vice-president.

Ronald Reagan and George Bush

Everybody expected the national election to be close. It wasn't. Reagan won by more than eight million votes. He won in all except six states and the District of Columbia.

Together after the election. Left to right: President-elect Reagan, daughter Maureen, wife Nancy, daughter Patti, son Mike and his wife Colleen, son Ron.

When he knew he had won, Reagan said, "I consider the trust you have placed in me sacred. And I give you my sacred oath that I will do my utmost to justify your faith."

Below: President Carter, with wife Rosalynn, admits to defeat. President-elect Reagan proudly shows a newspaper headline the day after the election. He won by many votes. Opposite: Ronald Reagan is inaugurated as president.

INDEX

(48)